ELIZABETH

MOON LORE

The Witches' Almanac, Ltd.

Address all inquiries and information to
THE WITCHES' ALMANAC, LTD.
P.O. Box 289
Tiverton, Rhode Island 02878

First Printing June 1997
Second Printing September 2002

Printed in the United States of America

Everyone is a moon, and has a dark side which he never shows to anybody.

—MARK TWAIN

I

MOON PASSAGE

Once long ago humans depended upon the Moon for reckoning time, planting crops and harvesting the sea. Its phases and its path through the sky were matters of concern and interest to all. Today very few people indeed are even aware, beyond a casual glance, of the Moon's presence. In a sense the lovely silver sphere which sometimes lights our darkness is more mysterious now despite the exploration of its surface. The Moon's curious forces continue to exert their influence over us and our planet. We and the oceans of Earth still unceasingly respond to the Moon's magnetic appeal. As a symbol of mystic significance, appreciated by so many ancient religious expressions, the Moon remains as potent as ever, at least to the poet, the artist and the witch.

Due to the nature of its orbit, the back of the Moon is unseen by viewers on Earth. This lends one more element of mystery to our single satellite. The Moon like the sun rises in the east and sets in the west. Unlike the sun, its size and shape continually change. Four cycles of approximately seven days each total a lunar month, which forms the basis for our present calendar system. The ancients held that the day began at nightfall, and the custom of celebrating holidays on their eve echoes the old tradition.

The slender crescent appearing soon after dark-of-the-Moon is called, obviously enough, the new Moon. It waxes, grows larger, to the first quarter visible in the sky as a half-Moon. The quarter in this instance refers to the sequence of the four phases. As the Moon waxes, its horns point to the east until it reaches full circle. The waning Moon diminishes in size, horns pointing west, until we see no Moon at all.

The times of rising and setting relate to the phases according to a definite pattern, as recorded in this old country rhyme:

A new Moon rises with the sun,
Its waxing half at midday shows,
The full Moon climbs at sunset hour,
And waning half the midnight knows,

NEW   First   FULL   Last
              Quarter   Quarter

THE SUN AND THE MOON

The simple fact that our planet has a single Moon to light the night and one Sun to warm our day has surely led to human conceptions of duality. What if human life had developed on Venus with no Moon at all? Or perhaps Mars with two tiny satellites, Saturn with nine, Jupiter with twelve—what themes and philosophies would evolve under such circumstances? Here on Earth we look to the Moon and Sun for inspiration and find duality. Forms recognized as male and female, good and evil, certainty and chance, instinct and reason have been dramatized in spiritual thought and the arts from the beginning of recorded time. And through these expressions we understand that all things involve their opposites and ultimately form one whole.

Ancient cultures paid homage to the Sun and the Moon as divine symbols and accorded both male gender. Sin, the Moon god of the Babylonians, ranked first in the spiritual world. Egyptians worshipped Khensu as god of the Moon. The Hindu Moon god Chandra rides across the sky in a silver chariot drawn by antelope-deer. His numerous consorts are the stars. In an environment where the Sun is a powerful and possibly destructive force, the Moon becomes a benevolent presence. Early male-dominated societies often chose to accord superior status and masculine gender to the gentle goodness of the Moon.

The Moon became a goddess with the rise of Greek culture. Certain aspects of her character are clearly drawn from the Phoenician Astarte and the Egyptian Bast, but Artemis was the first goddess of the Moon.

THE CLASSICAL MOON GODDESS

Anthropologists equate the importance of anything existing in a culture with the number of names by which it is known. The classical Moon goddess of the Greeks and Romans has more equivalent names than any other deity.

ARTEMIS. "She who hunts the clouds," is the original personification of the Moon, akin to the night luminary as her twin brother, Apollo, is to the Sun. The Greeks conceived the character of the Moon goddess in image and nature to be an ideal woman—a being worthy of worship. Describing her as virgin and huntress implied far more than mere sexual innocence and the pursuit of game. In classical Greek, the word "virgin" had a deeper meaning. It signified self-possession, dignity and compassion—purity as it related to spiritual integrity. Prey was not the object of the Moon's nightly quest across the sky. According to Greek thought, the Moon goddess hunted abstract qualities of hope, inspiration, goodness, and courage. Artemis came to be "the just and fair divinity who saves all from evil."

CYNTHIA. A name for the Moon goddess derived from Mount Cynthos on Delos, the birthplace of Artemis and Apollo. Homer tells the story of Leto, a beautiful maiden made pregnant by the sky god Zeus, and how she was denied refuge everywhere for all feared the wrath of Hera, wife of Zeus, who was enraged by his infidelity. Leto was finally granted sanctuary on the desolate isle of Delos where Artemis was safely delivered. Artemis, the poem tells us, then assisted her mother at the birth of her twin brother. The myth

provides another role for the Moon goddess—patroness of women in childbirth.

Friend of hills and woody places,
Goddess of three shapes and faces,
Virgin who, when summoned
Thrice by young wives in childbed,
Givest ear to the hard-pressed
And from death deliverest.

Odes of Horace

SELENE. The 3rd-century Greek poet Theocritus relates the myth of the Moon goddess in waning phase.

Endymion the shepherd,
As his flock he guarded,
She, the Moon, Selene,

Saw him, loved him, sought him,
Coming down from heaven
To the glade on Latmus,
Kissed him, lay beside him.
Blessed is his fortune.
Evermore he slumbers,
Tossing not nor turning,
Endymion the shepherd.

In one version of the myth, Selene persuades Zeus to grant her beloved one wish. Endymion chooses perpetual youth by means of perpetual sleep, and retires to a deep underground cave. In another, it is Selene who imposes everlasting sleep on her handsome lover. Whichever, Endymion must have been aroused on occasion, as all sources agree that he fathered fifty

daughters with the goddess. And when the Moon
wanes, it is said that Selene visits her lover deep in his
cavern of repose.

HECATE. The primitive Greek goddess of three realms—heaven, earth, and sea. The Moon before rising, after setting, and for the three nights when it is lost from sight belongs to the dark goddess of witchery, divination, and sorcery.

In ancient times, Hecate was represented as a single figure holding burning torches and crowned with a crescent Moon. Later, in classical Greece and Rome, she was symbolized as a triple goddess with three bodies standing back to back.

TRIVIA. The word may now be synonymous with worthless knowledge, but in time gone by it was the name Romans gave Hecate. Her triple-form statues stood where three roads met and so they called her

Trivia—*tri*, three and *via*, road. The crossroads, sacred to the dark goddess, suggest moments of decision.

LUNA. A Roman name for the Moon goddess depicted as a matron driving a chariot drawn by two white horses or sometimes, two young maidens.

DIANA. Originally the name of an Italian wood deity who became identified with the Greek Artemis, and like her, symbolized the Moon. The Romans celebrated Diana's Day on August 13th and it was the custom to choose a particularly fine tree and decorate it with her emblems: the crescent, bow and arrows, silver masks, tiny animal figures, scraps of bright cloth and locks of hair. A common gesture of respect used to address Diana in both town and country observances was with the fingers of the right hand clenched and pressed hard against the forehead.

DIANA OF EPHESUS. Evolved from a date-palm tree sacred to the Amazons, the well-known statue of Diana is decorated with a festoon of ripe dates. Historical sources mistakenly identify the dates as breasts and dismiss the primary significance of the figure. The statue is a tribute to the tender regard held by Diana for both wild and domestic creatures. From waist to feet are carvings of rows of animals—lions, rams, bulls, and deer. Cats climb to her shoulders and an ancient reference notes the crab engraved on her breast, "a creature sacred to her." Upon the original statue, the one destroyed by a Christian zealot in A. D. 400, a mysterious inscription appeared in three places: at her feet, girdle, and crown. ASKI. KATASKI. HAIX. TETRAX. DAMNAMENEUS. AISION. The lexicographer Hesychius, writing in the 5th century of the Common Era, preserved the words and translates them as follows: Darkness-Light-Himself-the Sun-Truth.

LUCINA. Roman goddess of childbirth, "bringer of light." Associated with the Moon as she governed the tides of the sea and gave moisture to the land ensuring fertility. Water is the element of the Moon.

CREATURES OF THE MOON

The stag, hare, and cat belong to the Moon. The elephant with its ivory tusks, the ram, boar, goat, gazelle, and water buffalo—all animals with curved horns or tusks—play roles in the lunar myths of many cultures. Folklore adds bears, wolves, swans, geese, night birds, bees, moths, silvery fish, frogs, snakes, crabs, and crayfish to the menagerie of the Moon. Luna drives white horses. Black hounds accompany Hecate. And the lion is one of the oldest animal symbols of the Moon goddess.

Ancient Egyptians often symbolized their deities in the form of animals, but the earliest representation of a divine figure in the company of animals belongs to the Phoenician earth goddess Astarte. Those rare humans gifted with the ability to communicate with wild crea-

tures have probably existed since time began. And if the original concept of the goddess Astarte was based on a living woman, we can imagine her soft voice and gentle manner as she tamed and tended the animals in her care. One thousand years later, Astarte's earthly qualities would merge with those of the Greek Moon goddess Artemis, for both were addressed as "The Lady of Wild Things."

English archaeologist W. M. Flinders Petrie collected art portraying Astarte from many sites and published the sketches shown here in *Decorative Patterns of the Ancient World*, London, 1930.

Herodotus, Greek historian and the world's first travel writer, visited Egypt in the 5th century B.C. and witnessed a celebration in honor of the cat goddess Bast. He likened her nature to that of the Hellenic Artemis, remarking on the dignity, elegance, and grace the goddesses shared.

SACRED RITES AND PRAYERS

We have no name for an ancient Irish Moon goddess, but it is evident there was one. Prayers to her, preserved by oral tradition, were finally written down between A.D. 600 and 1000 by Christian scholar-monks. Often disapproving of pagan subject matter, they nevertheless faithfully transcribed the earliest examples of Western literature—in existence long before the Celts invaded Ireland, long before the rise of Greek culture. The traditional prayers to the new and full Moons may belong to a society contemporary with Egypt's Old Kingdom, c. 2500 B.C.

Greeting to you, New Moon, kindly jewel of guidance!
I bend my knees to you, I offer you my love.
I bend my knees to you, I raise up my hands to you,
I lift up my eyes to you, New Moon of the Seasons.
Greeting to you, New Moon, darling of my love!
Greeting to you, New Moon, darling of graces,
You journey on your course, you steer the flood tides,
You light up your face for us, New Moon of the Seasons.
Queen of guidance, queen of good luck,
queen of my love,
New Moon of the Seasons!

O

Greeting to you, gem of the night!
Beauty of the skies, gem of the night!

Mother of the stars, gem of the night!
Foster-child of the sun, gem of the night!

Majesty of the stars, gem of the night!

From *Carmina Gadelica*, Vol. III.
Translation by A. Carmichael.

TO DRAW DOWN THE MOON

Thessaly is a pastoral region in northeastern Greece
long famed as the haunt of witches. Mt. Olympus,
abode of the ancient Greek deities, is in Thessaly. So is

the site of the inspiring Pierian Spring of the Nine
Muses, goddesses of the arts and sciences. Yet Thessaly
is primarily renowned for its witches. Their sorcery to
draw down the Moon has captured the imagination of
writers for centuries.

Sophocles and Aristophanes wrote of the Thessalian
witches in the 5th century B.C. Plato writes of them a
century later. Horace, Virgil, Ovid, and Lucan hail the
Moon-drawing charm at the turn of the Common Era.
John Dryden in 17th-century England described a
heroine whose "eyes have power beyond Thessalian
charms to draw the moon from heaven."

Today the phrase calls to mind a ceremony per-
formed by contemporary English witches in which the
High Priestess becomes the Moon Goddess incarnate.
A tape recording of this ritual inspired Margot Adler's
study of Neo-Pagans in America and gave her its title:
Drawing Down the Moon.

But there is another ceremony less well known and
similar in theme. This personal and simple rite is

probably closer to the original sorcery. Its purpose is to renew psychic energy, increase divinatory perception, and capture the elusive fifth element—the quintessence to nourish the soul.

THE RITE

At the time of the full Moon closest to summer solstice and when the Moon is high, go to an open space carrying a small bowl of fresh spring water. Position yourself so as to capture the Moon's reflection in the bowl. Hold it as steadily as you can in both hands for a slow and silent count to nine. Close your eyes and while holding the image of the Moon in your mind, drink the water to the last drop.

Chants to the Moon have been collected from the folklore of many lands. Examples like these kept the memory of the Moon goddess alive in the minds and hearts of those who sensed the magic of the divine symbol. Despite powerful forces determined to erase her worship by means fair or foul, their efforts were doomed to failure. The legacy of the goddess lives on.

Moon chants may be addressed to the full Moon or her waxing crescent in the west at twilight.

Pray to the Moon when she is round,
Luck with you will then abound,
What you seek for shall be found
On the sea or solid ground.

Luna, every woman's friend,
To me thy goodness condescend,
Let this night in visions see
Emblems of my destiny.

All hail to the Moon! all hail to thee!
I prithee, good Moon, declare unto me
This night who my true love shall be!

Gracious Lady Moon,
Ever in my sight,
Kindly grant the boon
I ask of thee tonight.

Revelation, XII, 1-16.   Albrecht Dürer, 1500.

That the feminine Moon shines only by reflected light from the masculine Sun was a prevailing theme in medieval Europe. In a detail from Dürer's Biblical woodcut, the goddess image crushes the crescent Moon under her feet; her hands no longer reach out in welcome. The powerful wings recall the celestial symbolism of a far distant past.

Moonwort

II

THE ASTROLOGICAL MOON

The characteristics assigned to each sign of the zodiac are based on centuries-old lore and legend. The Chaldeans identified the constellations in their present order as early as 2500 B.C., but it was the Greeks who in the centuries preceding the Christian era named the circle of animals the zodiac, who wove myths around the signs and bestowed many of the correspondences astrologers use today.

Cancer alone owns the Mansion of the Moon. All the ancient assigned qualities of this sign reflect the influence of the ruler of night—nocturnal, feminine, negative, passive, cold, moist, melancholy, and cardinal of the three water signs. These qualities easily interpret as the intuitive, emotional, mysterious and compelling personality defined for the Crab. Restlessness and a need to be on the move come from the Moon as well as being characteristic of a cardinal sign. Cancer's arrival coincides with the beginning of summer.

This woodcut by an unknown artist of the late 15th
century depicts a conjuror and his audience under lunar
domination. The goddess figure holds a torch and the
horn of plenty above a watery landscape.

YOUR MOON SIGN

The Moon's place in the zodiac at the time of your birth has a direct bearing on your instinctive behavior, habits, response to the environment in which you live, and inherited characteristics. We list below a précis of the key qualities each Moon sign holds.

You can easily determine your own Moon sign by consulting an ephemeris in your local library. An ephemeris will also provide the Moon phase at the time of your birth. In witchcraft a birth at dark-of-the-Moon is greeted with rejoicing. To be born at any time during a waxing Moon is regarded as a good omen, for the child will grow as the Moon does. Those born during a waning Moon are protected from harm by charms, amulets, and supportive ritual.

An Aries Moon at the time of your birth lends courage and recklessness.

If your Moon sign is Taurus, stability and bold determination are present.

To be born under the Gemini Moon foretells liveliness and versatility.

Sensitivity, tenacity, and originality are gifts of a Cancer Moon.

Leo's Moon brings with it strength, self-confidence, and creativity.

The Moon sign of Virgo bestows discrimination and meticulousness.

The influence of the Moon in Libra adds idealism and a bit of indolence.

When your Moon sign is Scorpio, you are proud, moody, and possessive.

A Sagittarian Moon connotes intuitive power and a certain restlessness.

Capricorn's Moon in your horoscope grants patience and a cautious nature.

An Aquarian Moon sign indicates humanity and a touch of eccentricity.

Imagination and a loving spirit grace those born under the Moon in Pisces.

LUNAR GEMS

The primary jewel of the Moon is chalcedony. Chosen by medieval metaphysicians as birthstone for the zodiacal sign of Cancer, the chalcedony is a translucent quartz varying in color from milky white to pale blue gray or warm fawn. An age-old occult use for the gem was to cheer melancholy spirits. Talismans carved from chalcedony were thought to counteract the dispiriting influences of the planet Saturn. The Romans wore the stone as protection against the ravages of the evil eye. Its waxlike luster calls to mind an image of the Moon, and many Gnostic amulets of chalcedony were engraved with the Moon's symbol. Seamen from all quarters of the Mediterranean cherished the gem as a protection from drowning. European folk medicine claimed the touch of the chalcedony upon the brow reduced fever, brought tranquillity to a troubled mind and speeded recovery.

Other treasures of the earth and the sea with strong lunar associations are amber, aquamarine, beryl, coral, moonstone, pearl, rock-crystal, and selenite.

PLANTS OF THE MOON

Herbal lore and legends assign certain members of the vegetable kingdom to the dominion of the Moon. Silvery foliage, pale cream, yellow, or bright white flowers; a cooling nature and perhaps other mysterious properties as yet undefined form the reasons why the following list of green growing things are said to possess lunar energy:

ADDER'S TONGUE - *Ophioglossum vulgatum*. An alien fern found in damp meadows and shaded woodlands. Its leaves have healing virtues and are most effective when gathered during the waning Moon. A single leaf imparts insight to its bearer.

CAMPHOR - *Cinnamomum camphora*. An evergreen tree, native to China and Japan, with aromatic wood and leaves producing a pungent substance widely used in medicine.

CLARY - *Salvia sclarea*. This garden herb's name is a contraction of "clear-eye," referring to the use of its seeds to heal eye irritations. Clary wine is made from its blue-white blossoms and has narcotic and aphrodisiac qualities.

CUCUMBER - *Cucumis sativus*. Slice a cucumber and the reason why it belongs to the Moon is quickly apparent. Probably of Asian or African origin where it has been cultivated for over 2000 years.

GARDENIA - *Gardenia jasminoides*. A native of China, grown in America since colonial days, its exquisite white flowers and lovely scent define it as a lunar emblem.

HONESTY - *Lunaria biennis*. Its seed pods called "silver pennies" are dried in the autumn for winter bouquets. An easily grown, attractive garden plant with fragrant flowers of white and purple, honesty belongs to the Moon.

IRIS - *Iridaceae germanica*. Although named for the goddess of the rainbow, this particular species yields the substance called *orris root* used in magical rites. Native to Europe, its lilac to white flowers have strong lunar associations.

JASMINE - *Jasminium officinale*. A night-blooming plant of tiny white flowers in the shape of stars with unforgettable fragrance.

LEMON - *Citrus limonia*. The fruit of the lemon tree provides the ultimate in cooling beverages. Lemons are used in witchcraft to counter ill-wishing and as guard-charms.

LILY - *Lilium candidum*. The Madonna Lily has been

cultivated for over a thousand years. Its pure white trumpet-shaped flowers bloom in late June to greet the sign of Cancer and the rulership of the Moon.

LOOSESTRIFE - *Lythrum salicaria.* A wild meadow glowing with the bright purple spires of loosestrife is a common sight in the northeast. Its alien seeds were carried to America in imported wool and shaken out to take root in the fields surrounding mill towns. Its link to the Moon may be as a mystic source of joy and inspiration, or even as a means to tame beasts as its name implies.

MOONWORT - *Botrychium lunaria.* An uncommon variety of fern found in dry meadows and northern hillsides. Its crescent-shaped segments in pairs along the frond are like tiny moons and give the plant its name. The alien wildling was brought to America by the colonists for healing fresh wounds and because of its magical reputation. According to folklore, moonwort opens locks and unshoes horses that trod upon it. Gather at full Moon.

MUGWORT - *Artemisia vulgaris.* The 18th-century Swedish botanist Linnaeus chose Artemisia as the genus name for silvery and gray-green leafy herbs. Mugwort was sacred to the Moon goddess in ancient Greece where it provided protection from evil and preserved energy on a journey.

NIGHT-BLOOMING CEREUS - *Hylocereus undatus*. A spectacular cactus of the tropics with large white flowers coming to bloom in June after dark.

ORPINE - *Sedum telephium*. A succulent with clusters of purple flowers blooming in late June. A maiden with romance on her mind is advised to "collect a single blossom of orpine in silence on Midsummer Eve and sleep with it beneath your pillow in order to dream of the man who will one day be your lover."

POPPY - *Papaver somniferum*. The opium poppy is native to Greece and the Orient. Although its narcotic properties can ease pain, fear of addiction precludes its use. Every source, ancient to modern, lists the poppy as a Moon plant.

SAXIFRAGE - *Saxifraga umbrosa*. A common rock-garden plant in England that grows wild in Spain and the mountains of western Ireland. Mounds of tiny white flowers display a kinship with the Moon.

SOUTHERNWOOD - *Artemisia abrotanum*. An herb praised by Greek and Romans for its magical qualities as a love charm. A strong and strangely pleasing scent comes from its leaves.

TREFOIL - *Trifolium pratense*. The perennial red clover, one of the sacred Celtic herbs, was held in high esteem by Druidic priests who saw it as a symbol of earth, sea, and sky.

WILLOW - *Salix alba* and *nigra*. The white and black (pussy willow) willow trees have long been associated with water and the Moon.

WORMWOOD - *Artemisia absinthium*. Classical myths recount how the goddess of the Moon presented this aromatic herb to Chiron, the Centaur who taught the healing arts to Greek heroes.

THE MOON AND SORCERY

Ceremonial magic draws its inspiration from the Hebraic Cabala and esoteric Christian doctrine. The Moon's affinities in the quest to attain supernatural power are carefully defined in the texts of occult literature—the *Grimoires*, or sorcerers' handbooks.

From the *Key of Solomon*:

Type of Operation

MOON - Travel, shipping, love and reconciliation, messengers. Theft (new Moon), visions, water.

The Effect of the Moon

Constructive efforts to be done when the Moon is new. Discord and hatred succeed when the Moon is waning. Invisibility and death only when the Moon is almost obscured.

Zodiac Signs of the Moon

The Moon must be in Taurus, Virgo, or Capricorn—that is, Earth Element Signs, for *Supernatural Effects*.

For operations of *Love*, *Friendship*, or *Invisibility*, the Moon must be in one of the Fire Signs: Aries, Leo, or Sagittarius.

Hatred and *Discord* is to be accomplished when the Moon is in a Watery Sign: Cancer, Scorpio, or Pisces.

All *Unusual Operations* are to be planned for dates when the Moon is occupying an Airy Sign: Gemini, Libra, or Aquarius.

THE POET AND THE MOON

Soon as the evening shades prevail,
The moon takes up the wondrous tale,
And nightly to the listening earth
Repeats the story of her birth;
While all the stars that round her burn,
And all the planets in their turn,
Confirm the tidings as they roll,
And spread the truth from pole to pole.

—JOSEPH ADDISON

The moon like a flower
In heaven's high bower,
With silent delight,
Sits and smiles on the night.

—WILLIAM BLAKE

O Trivia, Goddess, leave these low abodes,
And traverse o'er the wide ethereal roads,
Celestial Queen, put on thy robes of light,
Now Cynthia named, fair regent of the night.
At sight of thee the villain sheaths his sword,
Nor scales the wall, to steal the wealthy hoard.
O may thy silver lamp from heaven's high bower
Direct my footsteps in the midnight hour!

—JOHN GAY

The myth of the shepherd beloved by the Moon
goddess inspired poetry of enduring charm.

Opening lines of *Endymion*

A thing of beauty is a joy for ever:
Its loveliness increases; it will never
Pass into nothingness; but still will keep
A bower quiet for us, and a sleep
Full of sweet dreams, and health, and quiet breathing.
Therefore, on every morrow, are we wreathing
A flowery band to bind us to the earth,
Spite of despondence, of the inhuman dearth
Of noble natures, of the gloomy days,
Of all the unhealthy and o'er-darkened ways
Made for our searching: yes, in spite of all,
Some shape of beauty moves away the pall
From our dark spirits. Such the sun, the moon,
Trees old, and young, sprouting a shady boon
For simple sheep; and such are daffodils
With the green world they live in; and clear rills
That for themselves a cooling covert make
'Gainst the hot season; the mid-forest brake,
Rich with a sparkling of fair musk-rose blooms:
And such too is the grandeur of the dooms
We have imagined for the mighty dead;
All lovely tales that we have heard or read:
An endless fountain of immortal drink,
Pouring unto us from the heaven's brink.

—JOHN KEATS

The moving moon went up the sky
And nowhere did abide;
Softly she was going up,
And a star or two beside.

—SAMUEL COLERIDGE

I walk unseen
On the dry smooth-shaven green,
To behold the wandering moon,
Riding near her highest noon,
Like one that had been led astray
Through the heav'n's wide pathless way,
And oft, as if her head she bow'd,
Stooping through a fleecy cloud.

—JOHN MILTON

Art thou pale for weariness
Of climbing heaven and gazing on the earth,
Wandering companionless
Among the stars that have a different birth,—
And ever changing like a joyless eye
That finds no object worth its constancy?

—PERCY BYSSHE SHELLEY

Queen and huntress, chaste and fair,
Now the sun is laid to sleep,
Seated in thy silver chair
State in wonted manner keep;
    Hesperus entreats thy light,
    Goddess excellently bright.

Earth, let not thy envious shade
Dare itself to interpose;
Cynthia's shining orb was made
Heaven to clear, when day did close;
    Bless us then with wishéd sight,
    Goddess excellently bright.

Lay thy bow of pearl apart
And thy crystal-shining quiver,
Give unto the flying hart
Space to breathe, now short soever;
    Thou that mak'st a day of night,
    Goddess excellently bright.

— BEN JONSON

III

GOTHIC MOON

In occult doctrine, ancient and medieval natural philosophy, and astrology the Moon symbolizes the soul, the spirit, the unconscious mind and the unknown inner-self. Its shape, ever-changing, echoes the rhythm of nature in continuous patterns of growth, decay and rebirth. The Moon signifies change, transformation, and a light illuminating darkness.

The Moon's message reflects the rising spirit of the Renaissance, a rebirth of ancient philosophy, art, and literature in Europe. The invention of the printing press in the 15th century brought forth a treasury of lost wisdom. Gothic influence was still present during the transition as manuscripts of medieval metaphysicians became books. Works by Albertus Magnus, Cornelius Agrippa and others, separated by time and place, are remarkably similar in magical themes. A typical *Grimoire* or "Black Book," so called for the Church condemned them, sought to arm the reader with vital information regarding celestial requirements in the performance of ceremonial magic. Details concerning the Moon were part of every sorcerer's manual.

On the facing page, culled from a variety of sources, the Moon's symbol is the waxing crescent. The Cancerian Crab is more often than not, especially in the earliest examples, a crayfish.

THE MOON
Ruler of the first hour of Monday

Under the sign of
CANCER

Burn willow wood in a sacrifice to the spirit.

Powers of the Moon: policies, dreams, merchandise, travel by sea, lost love, theft.

Herbs of the Moon are chynostates (possibly clary sage) and martegon (moonwort) collected at full Moon.

Metal may be silver or platina (platinum).

Stones shall be pearl, crystal, spinel (balas ruby, a gem of pale rose red) or rose quartz.

Colors to be worn are white, cream, pale yellow.

Angels to address are Gabriel, Bilet, Missaln, and Abuzohar.

Sigil of the Angel Gabriel:

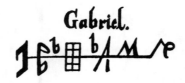

Talisman: Magic Square of the Moon, inscribe on parchment, use during conjuration of the spirit.

37	78	29	70	21	62	13	54	5
6	38	79	30	71	22	63	14	46
47	7	39	80	31	72	23	55	15
16	48	8	40	81	32	64	24	56
57	17	49	9	41	73	33	65	25
26	58	18	50	1	42	74	34	66
67	27	59	10	51	2	43	75	35
36	68	19	60	11	52	3	44	76
77	28	69	20	61	12	53	4	45

A magic square is an arrangement of numbers, none alike, placed in the form of a square where every row, column, and the two diagonals add up to the same sum. Of great antiquity, these devices were often engraved on metal or stone and worn as talismans. The renowned adept of ceremonial magic Cornelius Agrippa (1486-1535) constructed this magic square of the Moon.

When you're feeling angry or depressed, a brisk walk can often ease the tension. Mental exercise can turn the trick as well. Add each of nine columns vertically, horizontally and diagonally in your head without resorting to pencil and paper. The total of each column is 369.

Making a talisman of this Magic Square of the 9th Order will calm and discipline your mind for psychic work at the dark-of-the-Moon. Patiently place the numbers in numerical order from 1 to 81 in their correct positions on heavy white paper in black ink. You'll discover a series of patterns as you work which are fascinating in themselves.

TAROT MOON

Out of the Gothic darkness and of unknown origin, the Tarot cards of divination appeared. Partial sets from the two oldest decks exist today—one painted for a mad French king in 1392, the other commissioned by a wealthy Milanese family in the 15th century. The first printed cards were probably produced a century or so

later. The classic Tarot of Marseilles is a series of crude archaic woodcuts, images of surprising power.

The Moon card of the Marseilles pack is particularly rich in symbolism. Small wonder that the appearance of this trump in a reading is greeted with a shiver. The standard interpretation is one of illusion, deceit, darkness, and terror. Modern readers call the Moon the most dangerous card in the deck, for its malevolence is never lessened by the cards around it and only slightly modified when inverted. Some say the negativity is due to a definitive work written by the French Cabalist Dr. Gerard Encausse under the name of Papus. This volume, *The Tarot of the Bohemians*, Paris, 1889, exerted alarming influence. The theme that life on Earth is an evil condition from which the soul must escape is a dominating factor throughout the book. In such a philosophy intuition and imagination have no place.

The meaning of the Moon trump may be read as change, a shifting of thoughts and values. To perceive it ominous and evil is to accept a Judaic-Christian doctrine as outmoded as it is unsound.

The Return of Diana   Jost Amman, Nuremberg, 1578.

NEW MOON - White Goddess of birth and growth.
FULL MOON - Red Goddess of love and battle.
OLD MOON - Black Goddess of death and divination.

All hail to thee, Queen of heaven!
Thou showest two horns to mark six days,
And on the seventh will divide thy crown in two.
On the fourteenth day, turn thy full face unto us.

Seven is the Moon's mystic number, because each one of its four phases is completed in seven days.

Nineteen is a sacred number in Old Irish and Celtic lore, for the sequence of Moon phases within a single zodiac sign is repeated every 19 years.

The Mansions of the Moon, abodes of the soul, refer to the position of the Moon at noon on each of the 28 days in a lunar month.

Bow to the new Moon, especially the first new Moon of the year, as a sign of respect. It is courting disaster to point at the Moon at any time. Turn a silver coin in your purse or pocket at the first sight of the new Moon to gain good luck.

It is bad luck to see the new Moon for the first time on your left, or behind you, or through the branches of a tree. A new Moon on Saturday means foul weather. A full Moon on Sunday brings bad luck and toilers of the sea should not set sail.

The Roman astrologers of classical times considered the Moon sign of a horoscope to be of far greater significance than the Sun sign.

Marsilio Ficino, the Florentine philosopher of the Renaissance, defined the planetary image of the spirit of the Moon as an archer riding a doe, a huntress with bows and arrows, a little boy, a goose, or a single arrow.

Diana, goddess of the Moon and patroness of witches, was regarded as a demon by the early Christians.

Waxing: as the size of the Moon increases, its form takes the shape of the capital letter D: D for Daring. This marks a time for creativity, expansion, and development. You may glance up at the sky in the late afternoon to see the pale waxing half Moon beckoning. Later on as darkness falls, it shines like a beacon of hope in the west, raising your spirits and assuring the success of your ventures.

Waning: rising later night after night, the Moon diminishes in size, now assuming the form of the letter C: C for Caring. The time has come to relax, restore energy, and quietly dispel negative influences in your life. Banish fear, unworthy desires, and selfish motivations as the Moon wanes.

THE MOON AND THE WEATHER

Pale Moon doth rain, red Moon doth blow,
white Moon doth neither rain nor snow.

Clear Moon, frost soon.

A dark mist over the Moon is a promise of rain.

The full Moon eats the clouds away.

A new Moon and a windy night
sweep the cobwebs out of sight.

A red Moon is a sure sign of high winds.

And should the Moon wear
a halo of red, a tempest is nigh.

Many rings around the Moon
signal a series of severe blasts.

A single ring around the Moon that
quickly vanishes heralds fine weather.

When the new Moon holds the old Moon in its arms
(ring around the new Moon) disasters at sea occur.

Sharp horns on the sickle Moon indicate strong winds.

Blunt horns on a crescent Moon
presage a long spell of fair weather.

THE MOON AND MOTHER GOOSE

High, diddle, diddle,
The Cat and the Fiddle,
The Cow jump'd over
    the Moon;
The little Dog laugh'd
To see such Craft,
And the Dish ran away
    with the Spoon.

I see the moon,
    and the moon sees me,
God bless the moon,
    and God bless me.

Girls and boys,
    come out to play;
The moon doth shine
    as bright as day;
Leave your supper,
    and leave your sleep,
And meet your playfellows
    in the street.
Come with a whoop,
    come with a call,
Come with a good will,
    or come not at all.

THERE was an old woman toss'd up in a basket
Nineteen times as high as the moon;
Where she was going I couldn't but ask it,
For in her hand she carried a broom.

"Old woman, old woman, old woman," quoth I,
"O whither, O whither, O whither, so high?"
"To sweep the cobwebs off the sky!"
"Shall I go with thee?" "Ay, by-and-by."

FULL MOON NAMES

Students of occult literature soon learn the importance of names. From Ra to Rumpelstiltskin, the message is clear—names hold unusual power.

The tradition of naming full Moons was recorded in an English edition of *The Shepherd's Calendar*, published in the first decade of the 16th century.

Aries - Seed. Sowing season and symbol of the start of the new year.

Taurus - Hare. The sacred animal was associated in Roman legends with springtime and fertility.

Gemini - Dyad. The Latin word for a pair refers to the twin stars of the constellation Castor and Pollux.

Cancer - Mead. During late June and most of July the meadows, or meads, were mowed for hay.

Leo - Wort. When the sun was in Leo the worts (from the Anglo-Saxon *wyrt*-plant) were gathered to be dried and stored.

Virgo - Barley. Persephone, virgin goddess of rebirth, carries a sheaf of barley as symbol of the harvest.

Libra - Blood. Marking the season when domestic animals were sacrificed for winter provisions.

Scorpio - Snow. Scorpio heralds the dark season when the Sun is at its lowest and the first snow flies.

Sagittarius - Oak. The sacred tree of the Druids and the Roman god Jupiter is most noble as it withstands winter's blasts.

Capricorn - Wolf. The fearsome nocturnal animal represents the "night" of the year. Wolves were rarely seen in England after the 12th century.

Aquarius - Storm. A storm is said to rage most fiercely just before it ends, and the year usually follows suit.

Pisces - Chaste. The antiquated word for pure reflects the custom of greeting the new year with a clear soul.

Libra's Full Moon occasionally became the Wine Moon when a grape harvest was expected to produce a superior vintage.

America's early settlers continued to name the full Moons. The influence of the native tribes and their traditions is readily apparent.

AMERICAN	COLONIAL	NATIVE
Aries / April	Pink, Grass, Egg	Green Grass
Taurus / May	Flower, Planting	Shed
Gemini / June	Rose, Strawberry	Rose, Make Fat
Cancer /July	Buck, Thunder	Thunder
Leo / August	Sturgeon, Grain	Cherries Ripen
Virgo / September	Harvest, Fruit	Hunting
Libra / October	Hunter's	Falling Leaf
Scorpio / November	Beaver, Frosty	Mad
Sagittarius / December	Cold, Long Night	Long Night
Capricorn / January	Wolf, After Yule	Snow
Aquarius / February	Snow, Hunger	Hunger
Pisces / March	Worm, Sap, Crow	Crow, Sore Eye

MOON GARDENING

BY PHASE

Sow, transplant, bud and graft   *Plow, cultivate, weed and reap*

NEW	First Quarter	FULL	Last Quarter	NEW
Plant above-ground crops with outside seeds, flowering annuals.	Plant above-ground crops with inside seeds.	Plant root crops, bulbs, biennials, perennials.	Do not plant.	

BY PLACE IN THE ZODIAC

Fruitful Signs

Cancer - Most favorable planting time for all leafy crops bearing fruit above ground. Prune to encourage growth in Cancer.

Scorpio - Second only to Cancer, a Scorpion Moon promises good germination and swift growth. In Scorpio, prune for bud development.

Pisces - Planting in the last of the Watery Triad is especially effective for root growth.

Taurus - The best time to plant root crops is when the Moon is in the sign of the Bull.

Capricorn - The Earthy Goat Moon promotes the growth of rhizomes, bulbs, roots, tubers and stalks. Prune now to strengthen branches.

Libra - Airy Libra may be the least beneficial of the Fruitful Signs, but is excellent for planting flowers and vines.

Barren Signs

Leo - Foremost of the Barren Signs, the Lion Moon is the best time to effectively destroy weeds and pests. Cultivate and till the soil.

Gemini - Harvest in the Airy Twins; gather herbs and roots. Reap when the Moon is in a sign of Air or Fire to assure best storage.

Virgo - Plow, cultivate, and control weeds and pests when the moon is in Virgo.

Sagittarius - Plow and cultivate the soil or harvest under the Archer Moon. Prune now to discourage growth.

Aquarius - This dry sign of Air is perfect for ground cultivation, reaping crops, gathering roots and herbs. It is a good time to destroy weeds and pests.

Aries - Cultivate, weed, and prune to lessen growth. Gather herbs and roots for storage.

MOON SONGS

Shine on Harvest Moon • Carolina Moon • Blue Moon

When the Moon Comes Over the Mountain • Moon Song

By the Light of the Silvery Moon • Moon Over Miami

Moonlight Serenade • Moonglow • Moonlight Cocktails

Moon Love • Old Devil Moon • Moonlight Becomes You

Blue Moon of Kentucky • Say It's Only a Paper Moon

I Wished on the Moon • Full Moon and Empty Arms

The Moon Was Yellow • Moon of Manikura • Moon River

Moonlight in Vermont • But the Moon Got in My Eyes

How High the Moon • Allegheny Moon • No Moon at All

Fly Me to the Moon • Bad Moon Rising • Moon Shadow

Shame on the Moon • New Moon on Monday • Moonstruck

Moondance • Bark at the Moon • Dark Side of the Moon

By the moone we sport and play,
With the night begins our day.

—THOMAS RAVENSCROFT